CORFU CONF[IDENTIALS]

Out and A[bout]

This, the third Corfu Confidentials book, was inspired by the wonderful landscapes of Corfu and is designed to encourage readers to make the most of their time on this beautiful island. All opinions and indeed any mistakes are by own.

You will find a Google map to accompany the book here:
http://bit.ly/Corfuout-about

Follow us on our Corfu Confidentials Facebook page and our blog for more info and news on our other books.

Copyright © 2015 by G. Guy. All rights reserved. This book or any portion thereof may not be reproduced or used in any manner whatsoever without the express written permission of the publisher except for the use of brief quotations in a book review.

Contents

Introduction 3
North East Coast 4
North West Coast 20
Central 32
South 53
Index & Details 71

Introduction

In this series of books, I have been covering the questions I have been asked most by tourists over my last decade or so working on this lovely island.

In the first book, we covered the beaches, all 117 of them, in the second book we explored the remarkable Corfu Town in depth.

So now we come to the next question, what else can we do to explore and experience Corfu?

There is a surprising number of things to see and do on this relatively small island. I have hand-picked 66 of them for you, covering a wide range of activities, to ensure you can entertain everybody in your group, whatever your budget!

North East Coast

4. Antinioti Lagoon
11. Anthropograva Cave
12. Agia Trianda Monastery
16. Dimitris Horse Riding   Centre
18. Erimitis
19. Acharavi Folk Museum
25. Hydropolis
30. Kassiopi Castle
31. Panagia Kassopitra Church
38. Monastery of Agia Aikaterina
43. Nymfes Waterfalls
44. Old Perithia

45. Old Sinies
50. Mount Pantokrator & Monastery
51. Pyramid Adventure Park
52. S Bikes Mountain Tours
56. Corfu Trail – End Point
57. Dandalo Tower
66. Loutses Cave

Antinioti Lagoon

Walk to the end of St Spryidion beach, cross the wooden bridge and enter the area known as Nissos Island where you will find the lake. It covers 100 acres and it provides a home for fish, mammals, amphibians, reptiles and many rare birds, 96 different species have been spotted here in this protected area. A lovely place to walk around and commune with nature.

This is the lake mentioned by Gerald Durrell, in his famous books about his childhood on Corfu, "the lake of lilies" where the Durrells often picnicked.

Cave of Anthropograva

From the village of Klimatia along the road heading to the monastery of Agia Triada you will find these caves.

Apparently, it has some stunning stalagmites and stalactites and there have been discoveries here of pieces of archaic pottery and a Byzantine coin.

This one is for the serious cavers amongst you. Follow the stone path that leads to the entrance to the cave, where a 7-metre inclined passage inside the cave takes you to a bigger domed section with stalactites and stalagmites.

Agia Triada Monastery

A lovely little monastery set up high in the hills just above the village of Klimatia. It is worth going to look at this building which dates back to the 15th century for its remarkable murals which are believed to have been created around 1672. The other reason to make your way up here is the stunning views, across the north of the island as you can see right across to the Diapontia Islands in the distance.

Dimitris Horse Riding

One of the best ways to see the lovely area of Erimitis on the northeast coast is to take an hour out for a wonderful horse ride along the wooden paths and down to the beach.

Dimitris Horse Riding Centre in Avlaki was established in 2003 and is the only stables on the island made up entirely from rescued horses which is reason enough to visit them.

They offer rides suitable for all ages and abilities, so even if you have never been on a horse before I can recommend making this your first ride. Advanced riders can be catered for, just give them a call and they will fit you in.

The other bonus is that if you are staying in the local area they offer a free transfer service, so if not all of your group want to go, especially your driver, those of you eager to get out there can still enjoy this trek.

Erimitis

For those of you that like hiking and walking this area is perfect. Running from San Stefanos Beach all the way round the spectacular headland to Avlaki beach this area is perfect even for those who prefer more of a stroll than a march.

Currently, still untouched by tourism (although that is under threat) this area has several beautiful beaches, which only you and a few boating day trippers can reach and the three lake, surrounding wetlands and vegetation provide home to a multitude of wildlife, including over 200 species of birds and our friendly Lutra Lutra's, otherwise known as European otters.

Legend has it that the area gets its name from the story of a family that lived here 150 years ago. The beautiful young daughter was captured by pirates and taken away, leaving the parents bereft. The mother died from grief and the father became a hermit, 'erimiti' in Greek and so the name came about. The good news is that the story continues to say that the captain of the pirates fell in love with the girl and married her, and after many happy years at sea they returned and found the father and lived the rest of their lives with him in Erimitis.

Folklore Museum Acharavi

The work of a private individual, passionate about his home of Corfu and its history, this museum has a wide selection of Corfiot bygones, from an olive press to a shadow puppet show, from a water mill to a cobbler's shop, all tastefully displayed and helpfully labelled in Greek, English, German and French.

It is only a small museum, probably taking up only an hour of your time to wander around the room sets, recreating all aspects of traditional Greek Village life.

Hydropolis

This water park on the north coast is a good option if you have younger children, I would say 12 and under. Aqualand is great, but it is so big and busy that, in my experience, it can be a bit stressful with younger children as you can't let them out of your sight for a minute.

Hydropolis, being smaller and less inundated can be a good alternative. It is also a lot cheaper, especially on the all-inclusive days, historically Mondays and Thursdays, where the all you can eat buffet at lunchtime is generally good and a godsend for those of you whose kids love to eat. Drinks are included all day although the alcoholic ones are a bit rough! On other days, the snack bar isn't too expensive either.

So, if you are staying in the north of Corfu and want a relaxed couple of hours with the kids entertained, without spending a fortune, then head here.

Kassiopi Castle

Kassiopi Castle overlooks the fishing village of Kassiopi and was one of three castles which defended the island before the Venetian era. The castle formed a defensive triangle with Gardiki guarding the island's south, Kassiopi Castle the northeast and Angelokastro the northwest.

Its position on the north-eastern coast of Corfu overseeing the Corfu Channel separating the island from the mainland gave the castle an important vantage point and an elevated strategic significance.

Thought to be of Byzantine origin, not much remains today, despite some renovations and the track up is steep and not for the faint hearted. That said, there is a fantastic view from up there and you do get a real sense of history as you walk around the site.

Panagia Kassopitra Church

One of the most notable buildings in Kassiopi Corfu is the church of Panagia Kassopitra, which dates back to the 16th century. The church is dedicated to the Virgin Mary, and it gets its name from a temple of Kassios Zeus which once stood in the same spot.

The icon of the Blessed Virgin is said to perform miracles, the most famous of which was restoring the sight of a young boy who had unjustly had his eyes gouged out as punishment for a robbery. The beautiful building and its pretty surrounding are tucked away just off the main street and it is a worthwhile place to visit whilst you are in Kassiopi.

The church is open to the public but respectful attire is required, and there are many icons inside for you to see.

Monastery of Agia Aikaterina

This abandoned monastery is named after "St. Catherine" dates from 1713 and there are remarkable frescoes dating from the 18th and 19th century are preserved here.

To find it one starts from Saint Spyridonas' beach. After the wooden bridge of the sea lake there is a dirt road, follow this for about 1.6 km, roughly half an hour, until you come to a crossroads, on the left, in the forest of cypress and eucalyptus trees you will find this remarkable piece of history being reclaimed by nature.

Nymfes Waterfalls

Just outside the village of Nymfes, you will find these waterfalls. The road leading to them has been known to collapse on occasion so if you see any sign of this I recommend that you walk the rest of the way. They are situated in a beautiful wooded area which would be a great spot for a picnic.

Legend has it that the name of the village and waterfalls came from the fact that nymphs were seen bathing here. True or not, the best time to appreciate these falls is in the spring or from autumn onwards as obviously, in the summer months, they dry up.

Old Perithia

The crumbling ruins of Old Perithia, with its 8 churches and stunning location makes this Heritage Protected village worth the 9 km drive up the mountain to see. These days the road up is mostly good, with a few potholes here and there. The parking area needs work and is sloped, if it's raining I advise you park up at the top unless you have a 4x4.

It's hard to explain the charm of this abandoned village, perched just below the peak of our highest Mountain, Pantokrator. Dating back to at least the 14th century according to written records, this was one of Corfu's earliest and wealthiest settlements with around 130 houses all built by hand. At that time, pirate attacks were frequent so its location, so high up, was for defence reasons and a prime spot for lighting beacons to warn Corfu Town of approaching trouble.

Tourism and the attraction of the coastal areas gradually depleted Perithia, and many villages, of their population. Today you can wander around the remains of the village, admiring the old Venetian style buildings and stop for lunch in one of the tavernas that have popped up there. You will find some very good local dishes available up here.

Old Sinies

Another one for the walkers amongst you as the road does not go all the way up, and parts of the road that does exist has the tendency to disintegrate over winter.

Take the road up through Viglatouri village and go as far as you can. Old Perithia may be the famous 'abandoned village' but Palies (Old) Sinies truly is, not a soul to be seen up here and patently there hasn't been for quite some time.

You may spot some mountain goats or the occasional fox but that's about it. The views over the bay are magnificent and the buildings you can access, some are completely overgrown and reclaimed by nature, are interesting.

The atmosphere can be a little spooky, there are three churches, a threshing floor, tumbledown houses and stone wells.

Mount Pantokrator & Monastery

The peak of our highest mountain, whether you drive or walk up, at 917 metres is a reward in itself offering you the most spectacular panoramic views on the island. On a clear day, you can see mainland Greece and Albania to the east, the island of Paxos to the south and the three Diapontia Islands to the north. I heard it said that some days you can see the southernmost tip of Italy and although I have never experienced it myself I can believe it from up here.

The summit itself is covered with mobile phone masts and an absolutely huge pylon directly over the monastery which does detract from its beauty and sense of solitude upon the summit somewhat but doesn't spoil it entirely.

Once you get to the top and you have tired of taking photographs, which may take some time, you can pop into the monastery located here. The original church was built here in 1347 after an inhabitant from Sokraki village, apparently, found a marble column on this spot, with a representation on it of the Transfiguration of Christ. This inspired the surrounding villages to found the church, unfortunately that building was destroyed in the early 15th century, I haven't been able to discover how or why, but in its place, in the late 17th century the building we see today was constructed. There have been additions and restorations since then.

The interior of this small monastery is lovely, the Iconostasis screen is ornate and silver and the faded frescoes are said to be the work of the Corfiot painter Ioannis Tzilio. Outside there is a small slightly overpriced café for refreshments if you need them, but I would recommend stopping at one of the charming village squares and tavernas on the way down and have a real feast.

Pyramid Adventure Park

The rather grand name belies its size I feel, although it is a fantastic spot. This beachside restaurant and bar is in a lovely location with a nice section of sandy beach in front of it with sunbeds and waiter service.

Next to the restaurant is entertainment for the young ones in the form of Crazy Golf (€3 for the clubs, unlimited games), coin operated Go-karts, slides and swings.

The food and drinks are not cheap, but they are good and the staff are very friendly.

S-Bikes

If you like to get off the beaten path whilst on holiday and explore the countryside with a bit of adventure and exercise thrown in, then booking a tour with these guys maybe what you are looking for.

Well organised, friendly and with the up-to-date equipment, they are very passionate about biking and Corfu and their tours are great for all abilities as they adapt accordingly to what each individual can do. Taking in trails on the mountainside that you wouldn't normally get to see, this is a great way to experience this part of the island.

The Dandalo Tower

Another ancient ruin to be admired, set in the countryside up above the resort of Acharavi. Although only the walls are remaining, apparently, the current owner does invest money every year to keep back mother nature so it is still accessible. Built by the Doge of Venice, Enrico Dandalo to protect his newly acquired area, this enormous castle was three floors high and only accessible by a drawbridge. Part of the complex houses a small, single nave church which is still standing.

Loutses Cave

If you like a bit of a hike and are into subterranean geology than I can recommend hunting down these caves.

Follow the signs from the village of Loutses and when you reach a final parking area get your boots on for the slippery trail down to the caves. Full of stalagmites and stalactites and other weird formations.

I find the colours of the rock faces quite remarkable but the clamour of Rooks that tend circle the area are decidedly Hitchcockian!

North West Coast

9. Canal D'Amour

10. Cape Drastis

15. Corfu Brewery

17. Diapondia Islands

53. Sidari Waterpark Hotel

26. Ilios Jewellery Workshop

3. Angelokastro

22. George's Cellar

35. Mavromatis Kumquat Factory

6. Corfu Aquarium

48. Paleokastritsa Monastery

Canal D'amour

This stunning set of sandstone cliffs, caves and bays are yet another example of nature at work, the corrosion of the sea and the air forming this much loved and photographed attraction.

It does get extremely busy here, especially with couples trying to test the myth that surrounds these waters that if you swim together in the canal, you will be together forever. Whether you will be happy is another story!

Cape Drastis

Another spectacular feature courtesy of mother nature. These incredible sandstone cliffs offset perfectly by the surrounding turquoise waters are stunning.

The road up is extremely bumpy and parking is limited so it is better to either hike up there, not forgetting to take water with you, or hire a boat to visit the area. Slippery rocks lead into the swimming waters but the water is incredibly refreshing.

Corfu Brewery

Founded in 2006 this microbrewery has gone from strength to strength and is the first of its kind in Greece. Corfu Beers all belong to the category of Real Ale (a live product naturally brewed) whose fermentation and maturation take place in special vats over a period of several weeks with no stabilizers, artificial colouring or other chemical additives.

Their collection of 8 beers, including a 'blonde' pilsner, a 'dark' ale and even a Lemon Ginger beer have proved to be immensely popular.

Based in Arillas on the northwest coast they open their doors to the public on a Saturday, offering tours of the facilities and beer tastings.

They have also started a tradition of having an annual beer festival, each year embracing another countries beers' and culture. Held in October there are 5 days of tastings, workshops and entertainment from both cultures, a great experience for all.

Sidari Waterpark Hotel

This is a small hotel complex where you can use the pool area for free but there is a charge if you want to use the slides.

There are three bigger slides, a kamikaze fast slide, and 2 tunnel slides, (the one on the right is a bit faster) and some smaller ones for the little ones. It also has a children's playground, a covered games area with all the favourites such as air hockey, pool etc. and good sized swimming pools.

With the on-site restaurant and bar, lockers for your valuables, it has all you need to entertain the kids for a day, or two.

Ilios Jewellery Workshop

This interesting little place is based in the family resort of Agios Georgios, Pagi, on the north-west coast. Founded in 1996 by students of the Goldsmiths School Pforzheim, Germany, for the purpose of presenting their own work and the work of colleagues they now offer a workshop where you can make your own jewellery with tuition.

So, whether you want to make a simple leather bracelet from a shell you found on the beach or melt down your grandmother's earrings, that you'd never wear, to make something more suitable then check out this place.

A great, low-key atmosphere, right on the beach makes it worth spending an afternoon here.

Angelokastro

To my mind this is the most stunning of the fortresses on Corfu. The sheer scale of the thing and its location, 305m up on its rocky precipice it truly is a remarkable structure. Driving up the winding road from Paleokastritsa through Lakones and then Makrades (possibly stopping off here to buy local products in the shops that line the route) you finally bear left through Krini and approach the breath-taking view.

There is a small car park here and a café to refresh yourself after you make the climb, up the many steps, to the top of this monument. The view from the top is incredible, you can almost see the whole island from up here and you can understand why this was such a strategically perfect defence point for Corfu. Not once did this fortress fall in the many sieges laid against it. Neither the Genoan pirates from the west or the Ottomans from the east could break its defences, despite it being manned mostly by local peasants.

The exact date of its construction is not known but the first documented evidence dates it as before 1272. From the 14th to 16th century it was actually the capital of Corfu and the seat of the 'Provveditore Generale del Levante', governor of the Ionian islands and commander of the Venetian fleet, which was stationed in here.

From 1999 excavations and reconstruction were started on the then sadly decayed structure and 10 years later it opened to the public. As well as the stunning views, you can explore the Church of the Acropolis, the Circular Tower, the rather creepy anthropomorphic graves of the cemetery and the tiny, cave-like chapel of St. Kyriaki with its 18th-century paintings.

George's Cellar

This quirky little shop on the road leading up from Paleokastritsa to Lakonas is mostly famous for the family's hospitality but also for the home grown produce that they sell.

Sit and relax and sample their home-made wines, breads and olive oils, all of which are surprisingly good. Local herbs and honey are also available as well as the usual trinkets that you can buy as souvenirs.

A fun way to get your holiday gifts and savour some local character.

Mavromatis Kumquat Factory

As far as I know, Corfu is the only place in Europe to cultivate kumquats. They were first brought here from China by English botanist, Sidney Merlin, in 1860. The trees flourished here and so now you will find a plethora of products which you can spot by their neon orange hue.

The Mavromatis family started their factory in 1965 and now produce one million bottles of the liqueur, as well as jams and sweets from this strange little fruit. They also produce ouzo, brandy and other fruit liqueurs.

A visit to their showroom gives you the opportunity to learn about the history, production and the products that they make, as well as the chance to taste the various produce. And of course, the chance to buy gifts to take home, which as the fruit is said to help fight cancer, heart disease and hypertension, to name a few, might not be a bad idea.

Corfu Aquarium

Situated in the main parking area of Paleokastritsa, between two beaches, this little aquarium is a great way to spend some time, especially if you have children with you.

You will discover all about our local, and European, sea life from the helpful guides here. It is well maintained and when the fish get too big for the tanks they are released back to the sea and new ones are brought in.

Although it's called an aquarium there are also some reptiles there for you to discover and hold should you want to, including a massive Python and the ever-popular George the Iguana who steals the show.

Paleokastritsa Monastery

This small Byzantine Monastery dates back as far as 1228, however, the cells of the monks and the yard date from the 18th century. The setting is amazing, giving you panoramic views.

Be sure to look for the rock of Kolovri said to be Odysseus ship turned to stone by the God of the sea Poseidon on its return from Ithaca!

The monastery has a small ecclesiastical museum with rare Byzantine icons, holy books and other relics. This is a very popular stop for coach tours so it is best to plan to get there early, before 10 am or later, after 4.30pm so you can enjoy the peaceful atmosphere.

Diapontia Islands

Erikousa Island

The 3 Diapontia Islands off the north coast of Corfu mark the end of Greek Territory being just 40 km from the tip of Italy. This one is only 37 square km but has the largest population of the three, but as that's only about 500 people it never feels crowded.

To get there you can go by ferry, from Corfu Town, Sidari or St Stefanos on the NW coast. The ferry from town takes about 2.5 hours and doesn't give you much time there, about 3 hours, whereas the one from Sidari is only an hour and you will have four and a half hours. Ideally, you should look to stay overnight to really have a break but you will need to book well in advance.

August sees the influx of returning islanders who headed off to the States to live but make the pilgrimage back year after year.

The island itself is beautiful, sparsely populated and had a couple of wonderful beaches. There a few tavernas producing home cooking and lovely trails to walk and explore. It truly is an escape from it all.

Orthoni Island

Serviced by the same boats as Erikousa, Orthoni is the largest of the three being just under eleven square km. You can wander the cobbled streets of the main town, Ammos, with the traditional houses, restaurants and hotel, visit the old churches, the relics of the Venetian fortress and enjoy the enchanting view. There is also a lighthouse which still has the original reflector on the ground floor.

Mathraki

The smallest and least populated of the three it would only take just over 3 hours to walk around it. There are three beaches, one of which is 2km of sand which you can usually enjoy to yourself! Again, like its sister islands, this is a tranquil spot, full of nature and wildlife and great for walking around.

There are 2 tavernas and 2 cafes, the traditional one in Ano Mathraki in conjunction with St Spiridon church, mounts an annual festival on the Agios Spiridon saints' day 13th July. This is very popular with the local community and attracts many visitors.

Central

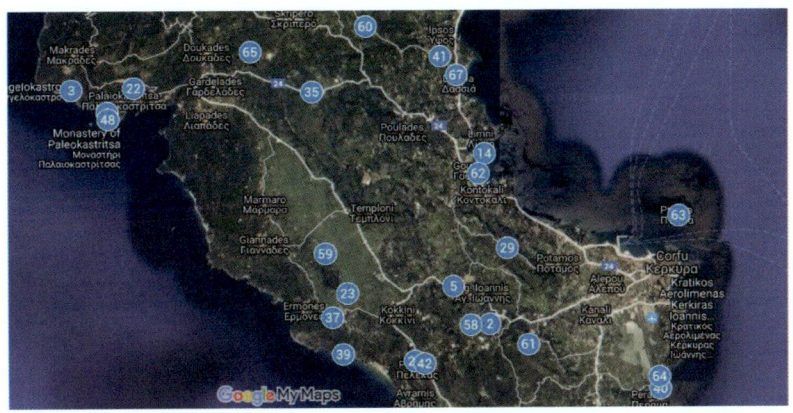

2. Ambelonas Vineyard

5. Aqualand

60. Trail Riders

41. National Gallery

14. Ipapantis Church

62. Venetian Shipyard

29. Kapodistrias Museum

63. Vidos Island

59. Theotoki Vineyard

23. Corfu Golf Club

37. MKB Honey

39. Myrtiotissa Monastery

28. Kaisers Throne

42. Museum of Traditional Costumes & Folk Music

58. Sivaland Riding Centre

61. Venetian Fountain

64. Vlacherna Monastery

40. Pontikonisi and the Monastery of Pantokrator

65. Corfu Donkey Rescue

67. Mountain Bike Shop

Ambelonas Vineyard

Nothing tells you more about a culture than its food, and here at Ambelonas you can get your hands dirty and experience cooking traditional Corfiot cuisine with the author of 'Corfiot Cuisine, In Search of The Origins', Vasiliki Karounou.

Learn about the history of the estate and be guided through the process of preparing and creating a 5-course meal which you and your fellow chefs will sit down and enjoy at the end.

It is an incredibly peaceful and beautiful location to learn about Corfiot cuisine.

Aqualand

What can I say about this place other than all the kids, big and small, will love it! It is one of the largest waterparks in Europe and in my experience, it is generally well maintained and staffed. From the huge wave pool to the 24m Free Fall Plus for the adrenalin junkies out there it has something for everyone.

The little ones are well catered for too with the Caribbean Pirate adventure pool and other areas designated for them. It is not a cheap day out, so it is best to make the most of it and plan a full day there and get there when it opens in high season to secure a sunbed or go after 3 pm when it is cheaper, if you can't imagine spending 8 hours of water based shenanigans.

If you know you will be badgered into going more than once during your stay it is worth getting the 2-day pass.

Trail Riders

This stables has been established since 1992 and offers treks for people of all abilities. Situated in the centre of the island their rides take you through woodlands, olive groves, vineyards and country trails.

Needless to say, you get some marvellous views along the way and after the hour-long ride cool drinks are on offer whilst the horses are being untacked and cared for. Suitable clothing should be worn, hard hats are supplied.

Apples and carrots are welcomed!

National Gallery

The Corfu branch of the National Gallery is rather oddly located in a sleepy little village. The building itself was originally a Venetian tower, which in the 50's became a hotel visited by many famous people including Aristotle Onassis and Maria Callas.

In 1993 it became the art gallery and is home to a superb collection of artworks covering the early post-Byzantine period up until the modern day.

With 150 pieces displayed over three floors, it really is a treasure trove and a must see whilst you are here.

Church Ipapantis

The much photographed Ipapanti Church of Christ stands in the sea connected by a 60-meter-long causeway. It was built in 1713 during the Venetian domination of the island of Corfu by a Cretan aristocratic family, who came to Corfu in 1669.

Originally there were precious art treasures in the church that this family had brought from Crete. After inheritance, the church came into the hands of different families and the church eventually became neglected.

Restoration of this church began in 1996. The three altar doors and four icons are 280 years old and were previously housed in the Byzantine museum.

Lovely spot for a photo opportunity, despite the surrounding area being a little down at heel, and worth visiting on saints' days for the ceremonies that take place here.

Venetian Shipyard

The Venetians chose to build their shipyard in this natural bay surrounded by material providing forests in 1716 as it offered protection from storms and possible attacks, although they also built a small fortress at the mouth of the bay to enforce this.

These days all that is left are the striking archways, the roof being entirely missing, but the sheer scale of the thing makes it worth stopping off for.

Interesting to imagine the huge fleets stopping off here for repairs and maintenance, a stark contrast with the modern marina just up the road.

Kapodistrias Museum

Corfu's most famous son, Ioannis Kapodistrias, the great politician and first governor of Greece is paid tribute to in this museum. It is housed in what was the families summer home which was donated by his grandniece, Maria Desylla-Kapodistria, who herself became the first female mayor in Greece.

The house contains furniture of the era and significant personal items of this interesting personality and you can discover more about his turbulent life, his time in parliament and his assassination by rebels in 1831.

Vidos Island

There is a small ferry boat that runs to the island during the summer months, and at only €2 for the return trip, it's a bargain. You can wander around the entire island, following the meandering, wooded trail habited by rabbits, pheasants and other wildlife. There are two beach areas and a taverna to enjoy, although these both become very busy in high season needless to say.

The history of the island is rich with drama; the Venetians reputedly built a tunnel under the sea to it from the Old Fortress to transport their convicted to the prison there, between 1537 and 1716 the Ottomans used the island as a base for their attacks on Corfu and during the 1st World War it was a sanctuary for the remains of the Serbian army. Due to the conditions of both the improvised medical facilities and many of the patients on the island, unfortunately, thousands died, hence the memorial found there today.

Another point of interest is a beautiful old house, which was used in the filming of 'Fedora', a 1970s-film set in Corfu and starring Michael York. The Island of Vidos has had many names over the years but this final name is said to come from the first name of one of its owners, Guido Malipieri, the Guido finally becoming Vido.

Theotokis Vineyard

This wonderful old vineyard is set in the lush and verdant Ropa Valley at the end of a winding road through some gorgeous countryside. As you pull up you will no doubt be greeted by their dog and maybe a goat or two.

It is worth calling ahead and arranging a tour and tasting if you can, although it is open to visitors every morning. The Theotokis family are an old established family, several members of whom have been politicians and their organic farming methods have made their wines and olive oils famous throughout Europe. Theotoki white wine is made from a blend of 10% Kakotrygi and 90% Robola, the red from Syrah and Cabernet Sauvignon and the estate produces 30,000 bottles a year. Famously being James Bonds plonk of choice, as he says in 'For your Eyes only' "I prefer the Theotaki Aspro".

Apart from wines, the estate also produces organic extra virgin olive oil from its more than four thousand trees, using traditional methods from start to finish at the estate's own press.

If you get the opportunity (and the privilege) to view the private library here, leap on the chance. It is an incredible collection of over

35, 000 books, maps and journals dedicated to history, art, religion and law of the Byzantine Empire, the Balkans and the Ionian Islands. A truly unexpected gem.

Corfu Golf Club

Now I am not a golfer, and I have never been to Corfu's club, so I shall stick with the facts and some feedback from those who have experienced it first-hand.

The golf course was designed by Donald Harradine in the lush Ropa Valley, incorporating the natural setting, and completed in 1971. It is an 18 hole course that stretches 6802 yards (6183 metres) and while not up to US or Portuguese standards, is one of the best courses in Greece. The fairways are good, with a couple of rough spots, and some of the holes are challenging due to multiple bunkers and water hazards.

It is open all year round and had a good Pro Shop and naturally, you can hire clubs and buggies.

If you want an enjoyable game of golf, with some challenging holes, in beautiful surroundings followed by a cold beer or glass of wine and a good lunch this is for you.

MKB Honey

There are many smallholders producing honey on Corfu, you will often see handwritten signs on the roadside inviting you to stop and try this marvellous local produce. The most successful of these has to be Panagiotis Vasilakis, who in 2001 decided to completely change his career and life and signed up for a course for new farmers and study beekeeping.

He now has 500 hives in 6 locations on Corfu as well as some on Erikoussa island and produces nearly 4 tonnes of honey a year. His plant in Vatos includes processing equipment, a chemistry lab and packaging technology and it produces certified organic honey, pollen, royal jelly and comb honey. Head here for a fascinating look at this age-old tradition brought up to modern standards and to sample some delicious honey.

Myrtiotissa Monastery

Nestled in the mountainside above the famous beach of the same name, you will find this lovely monastery which was built about 400 years ago, and takes its name from an icon of the Virgin Mary that was found in a cave among the myrtles by a Father Daniel following a vision.

Today another Father Daniel tends to the place, and he works tirelessly to improve the place with constant repairs and improvements but unfortunately very little cash, but it is his life work to bring the place up to scratch, encourage visitors and attract other monks to study there with him.

There is a small shop selling herbs and small religious items and Father Daniel is restoring the original oil presses here (dated 1896) so that the monastery and local farmers will be able to once again produce olive oil in the traditional way.

Kaisers Throne

So named, after Kaiser Wilhelm who when tired of the view from the Achilleion Palace would come to this spot to watch the amazing sunsets over the west coast and enjoy the panoramic view afforded from this point.

And who can blame him, it is absolutely stunning up here, especially on a clear day of course. I always forget just how breathtaking it is up here.

Located up above the village of Pelekas, with a convenient hotel terrace placed so you can watch the sunset with your favourite tipple, what better way to end your day of exploration?

Museum of Traditional Costumes & Folk Music

Located just before the hilltop village of Pelekas, is this wonderful, fascinating, private collection of costumes dating back to the 19th century.

With costumes originating from both Corfu and the rest of Greece, the collection has been created over many years by the museum's curator and is housed in her family home.

There is also a section dedicated to Corfu's musical heritage which is a big part of the character of the island.

Silvaland Riding Centre

Combining a riding school and a breeding program for the Skyrian Horses, a small-bodied horse that is believed to be a descendant of the horses that Achilles took with him to Troy.

Offering various levels of riding classes, events and different entertainment programmes throughout the year they work to raise money to fund their quest to improve the numbers of this endangered species of horse.

As well as their efforts to breed the remaining Skyros ponies, the Silva Project is also beginning work on a therapeutic riding center, an organic kiwi farm and vocational training program for people with disabilities, and a disabled-accessible tourist program for Corfu and other Ionian islands.

Venetian Fountain

This marvellous piece of baroque architecture was built in the 17th century by the Venetians.

The village lies on the crest of a hill and if you go to the top, not only will you have a magnificent view, you will also see a lovely old mansion, the church of Agioi Apostoloi, and the charming cobbled path that leads you to the fountain which used to supply the village with water.

Whilst you're in the village you can visit the private collection of Dimitri Paniperi in the cultural centre of 3,000 miniature cars no less, should you have the urge.

Vlacherna Monastery

If you have seen any photograph of this island, it will have been of this church, one of the most iconic spots on Corfu.

Attached by a walkway, which attracts many tourists with cameras, as it is sited at the end of Corfu airports runway making the view of flights coming in is quite spectacular.

The monastery itself, perched on the edge of Chalikopoulos sea lake, was built in 1685 and was at one time a nunnery. In the small cemetery you will find gravestones dating back to 1758.

From here you can take a small boat to Pontikonisi (Mouse) island.

Pontikonisi & The Monastery of Pantokrator

This tiny island with its even tinier Byzantine church is a big tourist attraction. During the summer months, you can get a boat from the nearby walkway and visit this little gem. There isn't much to see here and your visit won't take long but it is a pleasant little excursion if you are in the area.

I've heard it said that the island gets its name (which means Mouse Island in Greek) from its shape, I have also heard that its original name was Kondilonisi, meaning beautiful island, and it is derived from that. This island is another contender for the claim that it is the boat of Odysseus, turned to stone by Poseidon and also might have served as an inspiration for Arnold Böcklin's famous painting 'Isle of the Dead'.

Corfu Donkey Rescue

This wonderful haven started in 2004 and since then has helped and rescued hundreds of donkeys. Take some time out of your holiday, arm yourself with a bag of apples, and visit this wonderful place and support its cause.

You will be welcomed by one of the volunteers who can show you around and tell you the stories behind all the rescued creatures they have there.

This wonderful 'retirement home' runs entirely on the hard work of volunteers and donations so any help you can give is appreciated, you can even adopt a donkey!

Mountain Bike Shop

Probably the oldest established bike hire and tour outfit on the island. With a wealth of experience and a fantastic range of bikes, they offer tours and holidays to cater for all you adventurers out there.

Their friendly and knowledgeable staff will kit you out correctly before heading off for a scenic tour of the more rural parts of Corfu with stops in quaint villages for refreshments and to experience some local culture.

And don't worry if the going gets too tough for you, they have a van discreetly following the groups to pick up anybody who struggles and needs a ride for a while!

South

54. Sinerades Folk Museum

46. Tripas Taverna

47. Olive Museum

1. Achilleion Palace

27. Kaisers Bridge

7. Corfu Shell Museum

20. Folk Museum Kouris

24. Grava Gardikiou

21. Gardiki Castle

36. Mavroudis Olive Oil Family Museum

32. Corfu Kite Club

33. Lake Korrison

8. Bioporos Ecological Farm and Restaurant

13. Chlomos Village

34. Lefkimmis Salt Pans

49. Panagia Arkoudila Monastery

55. Corfu Trail Starting Point

Sinarades Folklore Museum

A rare insight into the way of life of a typical Corfiot house from 1860 to 1960 and well worth tracking down. The village of Sinarades itself is absolutely charming and worth a visit, do take the time to wander around whilst you are here. Once you pass the main square follow the blue signs to the museum.

The locals who work here are very enthusiastic and informative so it is worth having a chat with them and asking questions. Housed in a two-story traditional building there are many folk exhibits including things such as traditional costumes, musical instruments, agricultural tools, ceramics and much more to explore.

Tripas Taverna

Although this guide is definitely not a restaurant guide, I have to mention this place as it is almost a museum in itself. It had been run by the same family since 1936 and I don't think some of the memerobilia has been dusted in that time, but don't let that put you off!

Located in the lovely village of Kinopiastes, the family has been feeding and entertaining guests with charm and gusto all these years. The walls are packed with photographs of hundreds of visitors, including the more famous names of Anthony Quin, Jane Fonda, Sophia Loren and Jimmy Carter. Hard to imagine stars of this magnitude in a backwater taverna but they came in their droves.

The food is from a set menu, plentiful and very good along with pitchers of home-made wine. They have music and dancing most nights during the summer season and the place gets extremely busy so you will need to reserve a table. It is worth it for the experience and the ambience, let alone the satisfaction of your appetites.

Olive Museum

As there are over three million olive trees on Corfu and roughly 3% of the worlds olive oil comes from Corfiot olives, as you can imagine, olive harvesting and treating were once a huge industry here.

Not surprisingly then we have this museum, itself a working press until the 1970's and now an exhibition to show you all the equipment of the old mill, as well as the tools that were used for the harvesting of fruits and various other means for the production of oil and its uses across the years.

Achilleon Palace

The amazing and beautiful, if slightly kitsch, Achilleion Palace is located about 10 km south of Corfu Town on the edge of a village called Gastouri.

The stunning appearance of this stately palace takes the visitor back in history to when the palace was inhabited by two great figures from European history whose only common bond was their adoration for Corfu, Greece and its culture, Empress Elisabeth of Austria and Kaiser William II of Germany.

She built the palace in 1890, overseeing the entire decoration of the palace and it reflects her admiration and love for Classical Greece and in particular, the hero Achilles, who Sisy felt represented the spirit and soul of the local Greek people.

Perched on top of a hill and set in grounds that stretch down to the sea, the palace affords amazing panoramic views as far across as Corfu town.

Later, after her death, it was bought by Kaiser Wilhelm II, in 1907, to use as a holiday home. He expanded on the Achilles theme and commissioned the huge statue of a triumphant Achilles which bore the inscription "To the greatest of Greeks from the greatest of Germans" – but this inscription was removed after World War 2.

The palace has been a military hospital in WW1, an orphanage, a military headquarters in WW2, after which it came under the management of The Hellenic Tourist Organisation which leased it out in 1962 to a private company that turned the top floor into a casino.

The casino scene of the James Bond film For Your Eyes Only (1981) was filmed at the Achilleion.

Finally, in 1983 in reverted back to the H.T.O. and after years of rebuilding and restoration, the palace was finally restored to its former beauty.

It is now open to the public and is quite rightly one of the most visited, loved and photographed tourist sites on Corfu.

Kaisers Bridge

Kaiser Wilhelm loved the Achiliieon Palace as we know, but he wanted to be able to access the nearby beach at the bottom of its land easily and to be able to dock his boats and meet and greet his important guests without having to use public roads.

So he had this special bridge constructed by Carl Ludwig Sprenger, a German botanist who was in charge of the palace gardens, who stayed in Corfu until his death in 1917.

Parts of the bridge can still be seen today, although the central section was destroyed (ironically enough) by the Wehrmacht in WWII so that their artillery could be moved along the road.

Corfu Shell Museum

This small, private museum houses one of the largest collections of its kind in Europe and has been awarded by the IREDA Research Institute of Italy. It may sound like a rather strange museum but it is actually quite fascinating, started by Napoleon Sagias; a diver, shell collector and adventurer who lived in Australia for many years before returning home to Corfu in 1989, when he created the shell museum to show off his collection of over 10,000 pieces.

With everything from shells, of course, through to corals and embalmed fish and sharks this collection in really quite unique. It also contains one of the rarest shells in the world, the Cypraea Fultoni which is valued at €20,000!

This is a great spot to lose an hour or so with the kids on a rainy afternoon or if you just want a break from the sun. It is still owned by the same family and if the current owner Spyros Sagias is there you will be able to hear the incredible stories about the adventurer who started it all.

Folklore Museum Kouris

Another labour of love by a local, Spiros (of course) who has been collecting artefacts from all over Corfu for the last 25 years and housed it in this building by the new bridge in Messonghi. He has divided the museum into the relevant rooms of kitchen, bedroom etc. and even has a bakery and blacksmiths section all with original tools and clothing.

Spiro himself will give you a tour and explain the significance of the exhibits. He is also an artist and has some of his work on display that you can buy.

Grava Gardikiou

A little further up the road from Gardiki Castle, after climbing up through an olive grove, you will find this interesting but small cave, where tools, firestones and animal bones were found.

Archaeological investigations have shown that they originate from the Paleolithic Period, the Old Stone Age (20,000 BC). These are now housed in the Archaeological Museum, which hopefully will reopen soon.

Inside the cave, there are great rock formations for those of you that like that kind of thing and lovely views across southern Corfu for those of you that don't!

Gardiki Castle

The remnants of the Byzantine Gardiki Castle, the third defence bastion of Corfu along with Angelokastro and Kassiopi, are not as inspiring as the other two but still worth stopping off to see if you are headed this way.

This unusual building has an octagonal shape with 8, two storied towers in every corner and is believed to have been built at around the same time, and possibly by the same person who built the Angelokastro fortress in the early 13th century. Although you get a better perspective of its structure from overhead pictures, the interior is worth having a look at; on the parapets, you can still see the traces of the carvings and workmanship of the Byzantine craftsmen and interestingly there are traces of relics from other ancient temples embedded into the brickwork.

It is not known when and why the castle was abandoned, I would love to find out why, but it's said that when Barbarossa's (Ottoman Turkish captain and Admiral-of-the-Fleet) attacked in 1537 it was already deserted.

Mavroudis Olive Oil Family Museum

The olive is such an inherent part of our culture and life it is worth taking time out to discover a little of the history. This is an excellent small museum showing how the fruit of the olive groves in Corfu is transformed into fantastic-tasting olive oil.

The tour guide is often the owner, who takes the time to give hugely entertaining accounts of the whole production process, both historically and that used in the modern day. The old machinery is fascinating and clearly compiled as a labour of love.

The tour ends with a video of the current processes, followed by the opportunity to taste a variety of the oils produced here. And of course, it is available to buy and is marvellous oil, worth making space in your suitcase for.

Corfu Kite Club

If you like to try something new whilst on holiday, how about learning to Kite Surf? Based on the shallow and safe waters by Halikounas lake they have an ideal spot for taking you through the learning steps for this adventurous sport.

Courses available for absolute beginners through to more experienced customers and all the equipment is available to hire. They also have stand up paddle boards and organise excursions along the coastline.

And don't worry, if you are there as an observer the beach is fantastic and there is a great beach bar there to relax in.

Lake Korrison

The area surrounding this, our largest lake, is a nature lover's paradise. This sea water lake is located at the end of some rather bumpy tracks, in a protected area and attracts all sorts of birds on their winter vacations, including a wide variety of water birds, flamingos, swans and falcons.

Whether you want to discover the flora and fauna that abound here in this wild and rugged area or take advantage of the miles of sandy, remote beaches it is definitely an area worth exploring.

There is very little in the way of food and drinks available so it is a good idea to take a picnic. Although in the season you will find a small beach bar open so you can watch the magnificent sunsets with a cocktail!

Bioporos Ecological Farm and Restaurant

Another magical spot for those in the know. Bioporos farm, set in olive groves with views of Lake Korrison, is accessed down a long, and very bumpy track. This Ecological farm and restaurant is the dream of Agathi and Kostas Vlassis who bought the land here back in 1982, finally giving up their life in Athens and moving here in 1987.

The 70 acres of gardens and olive groves provide the produce used in the kitchen to prepare authentic traditional dishes, as well as the chickens who provide the eggs for the lavish breakfasts. Guests can join in all aspects of the farm life, see the pre-industrial farming tools and wander freely around the grounds. They produce olive oil, honey, seasonal garden produce, legumes, vegetables and herbs. There is also a horse, poultry, rabbits, bees, all of which are fed naturally. All in all, a great spot for families and singles alike, guaranteed a relaxing time and a huge Greek welcome.

The restaurant is currently undergoing renovations and is set to reopen for April 2017. Weekends only April and May then every day through to the end of October.

Chlomos Village

Corfu has many charming old villages to visit and this is one of them. Perched up on a hill at an altitude of 270m it affords you wonderful views of the surrounding countryside and the sea.

This wonderful old village is well preserved, with its crazy paving streets, colourful houses and typical Venetian architecture built around the main square.

With a couple of tavernas and a wonderful little art shop called 'Ionios Anemos Workshop' where everything is handmade from recycled materials, it is definitely worth stopping here for a lunch break and to enjoy the views.

Lefkimmis Salt Pans

Now disused and returning to their natural state, there are still signs of the previous flourishing salt industry that went on here, dating back to the 15th century, in the form of abandoned, rusting machinery - buckets, scoops and wheeled carts. It is now known as a nature reserve and a popular spot for birdwatchers.

Here you will also find the small church of Agios Ioannis and the first ever floating lighthouse in Greece which was built in 1825.

Panagia Arkoudila Monastery

Not far from the throbbing nightlife of Kavos is a beautiful, scenic, wooded area, Arkoudila Woods where you will find, perched up on the hills the remains of this monastery dating back to 1710. It's another lovely walk with excellent photo opportunities along the way, follow the signs from Spatera.

Being so close to cliffs at the southern tip of the island the monastery had to protect itself from attacks and there was a tunnel that used to run from the eastern tower all the way down to the beach so they could escape if needs be. During World War 2 it was used as a fortified firing position by the Greek army, hard to imagine now in such a peaceful setting.

There are some altars set up by one of the gateways where you could light a candle if you have the foresight to bring one with you and say a prayer for your nearest and dearest.

The Corfu Trail

This wonderful trail takes the keen walkers amongst you along paths that span the length of the island for 220km.

Starting at the Cape of Aspro Kavos in the south and avoiding the main roads, it takes you on an adventure through olive groves, mountains and beaches, showing you the non-commercial side of the island.

The path is strategically waymarked with yellow signs and arrows which are renewed every couple of years, so hopefully they will still be in place when you take this route.

To make the most of the trail, check out their website and guide on the site listed in the index.

Index & Details

Acharavi Folk Museum 9

Tel: +30 26630 63052 Fee: €3/€1.50 Open: Monday – Saturday 10am – 2pm Website: http://www.museum-acharavi.com/

Achilleion Palace 58

Tel: +30 26610 56210 Fee: €8 Open: 08:00-19:00 Mon-Fri/ Saturday, Sunday 08:00-14.30 Website: http://www.achillion-corfu.gr/default_en.html

Agia Trianda Monastery 6

Ambelonas Vineyard 34

Tel: +30 693 215 8888 Fee: Varies, contact for details Website: http://ambelonas-corfu.gr/

Angelokastro 26

Open: 10 – 3, Tues – Sun Fee: €3

Anthropograva Cave 5

Antinioti Lagoon 5

Aqualand 35

Tel: +30 2661058351 Open:May – October 10am – 6pm Fee: €27/€19 5-12yrs Website: http://www.aqualand-corfu.com/

Bioporos Ecological Farm and Restaurant 67

Tel: +30 26610 76224

Website: - http://www.bioporos.gr

Canal D'Amour 21

Cape Drasti 22

Chlomos Village 68

Corfu Aquarium 29

Tel: +30 26630 41339 Open: 10 – 6pm Fee: €6/4 Website: http://www.corfuaquarium.com

Corfu Brewery 23

Tel: 2663 052072 Open: Contact for details Website: http://www.corfubeer.com/

Corfu Donkey Rescue 52

Tel: +30 6947375992 Open: Contact for details Website: +30 6947375992

Corfu Golf Club 43

Tel: +30 2661 094220 Open: 8am – 8pm Fee: Various Website: http://corfugolfclub.com/

Corfu Kite Club 65

Tel: +30 6945769280 Open/Fees: Contact for details Website: http://www.kite-club-corfu.com/

Corfu Shell Museum 60

Tel: +30 2661 072227 Open 10 – 7pm May to October Fee: €4/€2

Corfu Trail Starting Point 71

http://corfutrailguide.com/

Dandalo Tower 19

Diapondia Islands 31

From Corfu City Port - Boat Schedules: +30-26610-40002/26610 26314

From Agios Stefanos NW Port - +30 26613 65200/+30 69324 45395

From Sidari (ferry Nearhos): Tuesday-Wednesday-Saturday-Sunday at 09:30 and arrives at 10:20

Dimitris Horse Riding Centre 7

TEL: +30 6973328513 – May-Oct RIDES: 9am/11am/5pm Fee: From €25 p/p Website: http://www.dimitriscorfu.gr/

Erimitis 8

Folk Museum Kouris 61

Tel: +30 698 844 7798 Open: Contact for details Fee: €3

Gardiki Castle 63

George's Cellar 27

Tel: +30 695 1000 817 Open: 9am – 9pm May - Oct

Grava Gardikiou 62

Hydropolis 9

Tel: +30 26630 64000 Open: 10 – 6pm Fee: €15/€11 Standard Entry Website: http://gelinavillage.gr/en/hydropolis/

Ilios Jewellery Workshop 25

Tel: +30 2663 096043 Open: April – Oct Fee: Contact for details - ilios@ilios-living-art.com

Ipapantis Church 38

Kaisers Bridge 59

Kaisers Throne 46

Kapodistrias Museum 40

Tel: +30 2661 039528 Open daily except Monday – 10 – 2pm Fee:

Kassiopi Castle 9

Lake Korrison 66

Lefkimmis Salt Pans 69

Loutses Cave 20

Mavromatis Koumquat Factory 28

Tel: +30 26630 22174 Open: Daily – Contact for details Website: http://kumquat.gr/

Mavroudis Olive Oil Family Museum 64

Tel: +30 2661 076759 Open: daily, various Fee: Contact for details

MKB Honey 44

Tel: +30 26610 95148 Website: http://www.mrhoney.eu

Monastery of Agia Aikaterina 12

Mount Pantokrator & Monastery 16

Mountain Bike Shop 53

Tel: +30 26610 93344 Open & Fee: Various Check Website: http://www.mountainbikecorfu.gr/

Museum of Traditional Costumes & Folk Music 47

Tel: +30 6932515421 Open: 10-2 daily Fee: €2

Myrtiotissa Monastery 45

Tel: +30 26610 94301 Website: http://www.mirtidiotissa.com/

National Gallery 37

Tel: +30 26610-93333 – Open:Monday / Thursday / Saturday / Sunday:08.30 - 15.30

Wednesday / Friday: 10.00 - 14.00 and 18.00 - 21.00 Tuesday: closed

Fee: 2 €: 1€ Website: http://www.nationalgallery.gr/ Under Annexes

Nymfes Waterfalls 13

Old Perithia 14

Old Sinies 15

Olive Museum 57

Tel: +30 26613 61800 - Fee: Free Open: Contact for details

Paleokastitsa Monastery 30

Tel: +30 2662 041210 Open: Daily - Closed between 1-3 – Contributions Welcome

Panagia Arkoudila Monastery 70

Panagia Kassopitra Church 11

Pontikonisi and the Monastery of Pantokrator 51

Boats run daily May – Oct – Every 30 mins - €2 p/p

Pyramid Adventure Par 17k

Tel: +30 266 3098 495 Open: May – October Website: https://www.corfupyramid.com/

S Bikes Mountain Tours 18

Tel: +30 2663 064115 Open: 9 – 7pm Mon – Sat – Fee: Various Website: http://www.corfumountainbikes.com/

Sidari Waterpark Hotel 24

Tel: +30 2663 099066 Open: May - Oct Fee: €5 p/p for the day €10 unlimited access Website: http://www.sidariwaterpark.com/

Sinerades Folk Museum 55

Tel: +30 26610-54962 Open: Tues – Sun 9.30 – 2pm Fee: €2

Sivaland Riding Centre 48

Tel: +30 26610 52492 +30 694 700 4784 Website: http://silvaland.wixsite.com/corfu

Theotoki Vineyard 42

Tel: +30 694 559 3016 Open 10 – 3pm Website: http://www.theotoky.com/

Trail Riders 36

Tel: + 30 6946 653 317 Call for details Website: http://www.trailriderscorfu.com/

Tripas Taverna 56

Tel: +30 2661 056333 Call for reservations Website: http://www.tripas.gr/

Venetian Fountain 49

Venetian Shipyard 39

Vidos Island 41

Boats run from the old port: May – Oct on the hour, return on the half hour - €2 return

Vlacherna Monastery 50

Photo Credits

Angelokastro – By Dr.K. – Own work, CC BY-SA 3.0, https://commons.wikimedia.org/w/index.php?curid=15706054

Achillieon – Kurt Bauschardt – https://www.flickr.com/photos/kurt-b/17229712521

Lake Antonisi – Polly Tunnel https://creativecommons.org/licenses/by-sa/4.0/deed.en Wikimedia Commons

Aqualand – Brian 'Donovan - https://www.flickr.com/photos/odonovan/3868746402

Bioporos – Curtesy of Bioporos

Canal D'amour – Sellenl - https://www.flickr.com/photos/ellensln/7230495884

Cape Drastis – Luc.T - https://www.flickr.com/photos/luctnl/16635062394

Grava Gardikiou – Muffinn - https://www.flickr.com/photos/mwf2005/17260326446

Chlomos – Dimitris Kamaras - https://www.flickr.com/photos/127226743@N02/28550852284

Church Ipapantis – Angel Hernanseaz - https://www.flickr.com/photos/ahernansaez/2889041121

Corfu Beer – Luc Coekaerts - https://www.flickr.com/photos/luc_coekaerts/26676788665

Trail Riders – Kat Sommers - https://www.flickr.com/photos/katsommers/3790451428

Dimitrls Horse Ring – Curtesy of Dimitris Horse Riding – http://www.dimitriscorfu.gr

Corfu Donkey sanctuary – curtesy of their website - http://www.corfu-donkeys.com/

Erikoussa – Matt Lucht - https://www.flickr.com/photos/mattlucht/4841079618/

Gardiki Castle – Jennifer Slot - https://www.flickr.com/photos/jennifurr-jinx/1385177417

Hydropolis – Danial H - https://www.flickr.com/photos/hueneborg/15378786312

Ilios - https://www.facebook.com/ilioslivingart/

Kassiopi Castle – Matt Lucht - https://www.flickr.com/photos/mattlucht/4840460377 - Cropped

Kassiopi Church – Petr Aust - https://www.flickr.com/photos/petraust/9438499014/

Kite Surfing – Muffinn - https://www.flickr.com/photos/mwf2005/17297762301

Lake Korrison – Kurt Bauschardt - https://www.flickr.com/photos/mwf2005/17297762301

Mavromatis Kumquat – Muffinn - https://www.flickr.com/photos/mwf2005/17102601650

Vlacherna Monastery – Vince Smith - https://www.flickr.com/photos/vsmithuk/8717003308

Paleokastritsa Monastery – Petr Aust - https://www.flickr.com/photos/petraust/9454949401

Pantokrator – William Warby https://www.flickr.com/photos/wwarby/30010281823

Cover William Warby - https://www.flickr.com/photos/wwarby/30527023252

Mouse Island – Muffinn - https://www.flickr.com/photos/mwf2005/17298148655

Old Perithia – Predrag Stojadinovic - https://www.flickr.com/photos/stojadinovicp/19780962879/

Pyramid Adventure Park - http://www.pyramidcitycorfu.com/adventurepark.php

S-Bikes - http://www.corfumountainbikes.com/

Theotokis Vineyard - http://www.theotoky.com/

Vidos – Marco Spaarpen - https://www.flickr.com/photos/marcusspaapen/4950995078

Venetian Shipyard – Muffinn - https://www.flickr.com/photos/mwf2005/17292549271

Corfu Trail – Luc Coekaerts - https://www.flickr.com/photos/luc_coekaerts/26403118770/

Printed in Great Britain
by Amazon